VINTAGE RUSSIAN

VINTAGE RUSSIAN

Props and Jets of the Iron Curtain Airlines

Colin Ballantine

Airlife
England

Front Cover

Top:
Interflug Tupolev Tu-124 roars away from Berlin-Schönefeld Airport in August 1974.

Centre left:
The Antonov Design Bureau's demonstration An-26, wearing Aeroflot colours, prepares to land at the 1975 Paris Air Show.

Centre right:
At the 1975 Paris Air Show, CCCP-77144 represents the Soviet Union's supersonic airliner, seen in a slow fly-past with its 'ears' fully extended.

Below left:
By far the world's biggest helicopter, the Mil Mi-12, made its only appearance in the west at the 1971 Paris Air Show.

Below right:
Portrait of a classic, the Antonov An-2 as an Aeroflot VIP version at Berlin-Schönefeld, August 1978.

Back cover
The beautiful lines of the Tupolev Tu-114 can be appreciated in this portrayal of CCCP-76470 at Brussels during October 1966.

Copyright © 1998 Colin Ballantine
First published in the UK in 1998
by Airlife Publishing Ltd

British Library Cataloguing-in-Publication Data
A catalogue record for this book
is available from the British Library

ISBN 1 85310 971 1

This book contains rare, early colour photographs and the Publisher has made every endeavour to reproduce them to the highest quality. Some, however, have been technically impossible to reproduce to the standard that we normally demand, but have been included because of their rarity and interest value.

Typeset by Phoenix Typesetting, Ilkley, West Yorkshire, England.
Printed in Hong Kong.

Airlife Publishing Ltd
101 Longden Road, Shrewsbury, SY3 9EB, England

Acknowledgements

In my extensive travels in search of Soviet-built airliners, many aircraft have been seen and not photographed. The airport authorities made it quite clear what was forbidden to be photographed and what was permitted. I was not prepared to dispute this on the ramp of their airport in a foreign country. Consequently many airliners escaped my camera. Somewhere, sometime, someone will eventually capture these airliners on film and fortunately I have a circle of friends who were able to fill a few missing gaps of airliners for this book. I can always rely on Tom Singfield to dig deep into his collection for a few slides of the 'ones that got away'. The same goes for Christian Volpati and Dr Jean Magendie, both of France. My grateful thanks go to these friends.

A special thanks must also go to Airlife Publishing for their continued confidence in producing books on the fascinating subject of Soviet-built transport aircraft.

Introduction

This nostalgic review of *Vintage Russian* airliners, covers the period of the true 'Cold War' years of the mid-1950s to 1980. A few exceptions of rare airliners in the post-1980 era have also been included.

During the 1950s and 1960s, airlines operating Russian-built airliners frequently failed to appear at their destinations due to low patronage or maintenance problems. In addition, during this period tourism in Communist countries was non-existent, therefore the demand for passenger seats was low. Generally speaking, the patrons were official businessmen and diplomats who suffered from an in-built fear of flying when they saw their Ilyushin Il-14 radial piston-engined airliner splutter into life and groan to the end of the runway for their epic flight. The other type of passenger was a very small group of aircraft enthusiasts (who could be counted on one hand) that were game enough to clamber onboard anything Russian-built that was flying east, to see what was behind the 'iron curtain'.

Recalling many of these early eastbound visits, I was anxious to update my private records of the aviation scene in these inhospitable areas of the world, and after a few test visits realised this was a dangerous business. However, through this book I am able to share the vintage days of Soviet aviation. This era passed without farewell, unlike in the western world where the last flight of a certain type of airliner was recorded in great detail with no shortage of passengers to proudly declare in future years that they flew on the last commercial Viscount, Comet or whatever; the Soviet-style system was a non-event and passed without mention.

The propeller and early jet era of Soviet-built airliners was indeed an interesting one. The early post-war years saw the famous DC-3 Dakota infiltrate the Communist Bloc countries as the Russian-built Lisunov Li-2, a reliable aircraft that enjoyed many years of service flying alongside the Ilyushin Il-12 and Il-14; these three airliners became the backbone of many airline fleets throughout the 1950s.

During the late-1950s three Soviet-built airliners made their maiden flights and went on to become Soviet 'classics'. The four-engined turboprop Ilyushin Il-18, similar to the Vanguard and Britannia provided comfortable seating for 100-plus passengers with a considerably greater range than its predecessor, the Il-14. Next came the world's first jetliner, the twin-engined Tupolev Tu-104, similar to the British Comet. Both jets from the same era had their own characters and both types were retired about the same time in the early-1980s. The third in this trio of classics was the Tupolev Tu-114, a four-engined contra-rotating propeller airliner of enormous proportions that could cruise at the same speed as a modern jet airliner which for a turboprop airliner was phenomenal.

The early 1960s saw the development of the Tu-124 which was designed as a smaller version of the Tu-104 and used as an interim airliner until the introduction of the Tu-134 some three years later. As the jet era gained momentum, the four-engined Vc-10-style Ilyushin Il-62 took to the air as a replacement for the giant Tu-114.

The Antonov Design Bureau was also busy making its mark in Soviet aviation history. During the early 1960s the Antonov An-24 appeared, followed by a production-run of over a thousand. The Antonov production plant at Kiev produced the world's largest cargo aircraft, the An-22. Like the Tu-114, it too had four engines and contra-rotating props. Its carrying capacity was a staggering 80,000 kilos.

Most of the Soviet-built classic airliners have long since gone; however, if you have the time and money these classics can be viewed in museums in countries that were once aligned with the Soviet Union.

Many of the colour slides featured in this book are old and were shot with poor equipment that can only be described as forerunners of today's high tech photographics, so please excuse the quality, it was the best available at the time.

Throughout these pages can be seen some very rare vintage Soviet airliners and helicopters operating in their prime days as revenue-earning aircraft. Most of these classics have either been scrapped or crashed many years ago, the only evidence available in this modern age of high tech airliners is a box of ageing transparencies that have now become *Vintage Russian*.

Thousands of Antonov An-2s have been operated by Aeroflot since 1947 as an extremely versatile and unique biplane. The sound of its 1,000-hp Shvetsov radial engine always commands the utmost attention as does its very short take-off capability. During the 1960s and 1970s, sightings were rare in the western world, however, they were found in large numbers in eastern Europe. CCCP-07758 visited Berlin-Schönefeld Airport in August 1978, where it was photographed. This particular aircraft was fitted with six luxury leather seats, fitted carpets and window curtains. The unusual colour scheme was freshly painted and as a luxury VIP version the overall look of the aircraft was much better than the current standard colours.

Left:
DM-SKC was one of twenty-five Kiev-built An-2s operated by Deutsche Lufthansa, all of which were transferred to Interflug in 1963. Most of the fleet were fitted with large rectangular windows, and operated passenger services throughout East Germany until 1965 when they were replaced by seven An-24s. DM-SKC was manufactured in 1957, withdrawn from use around 1969 and broken up for spares in August 1975 at Berlin-Schönefeld Airport. This rare colour picture shows DM-SKC in its original form at Berlin-Schönefeld in September 1962.

Below:
The standard An-2s of Aeroflot used as crop sprayers usually wore the sandy colours on the fuselage with pale blue wings. CCCP-40718 prepares to take-off from MladáBoleslav, Czechoslovakia in July 1977 on a spray training flight.

Throughout the 1960s a small number of Aeroflot An-12 freighters visited the airports of western Europe. Most examples proudly displayed the old red colours of Aeroflot and a sinister-looking tail bullet bearing a cannon-gun nest. A slight variation of this version was the genuine civilian freighter with the armament removed and the nest completely blanked off. One such civilian freighter that visited London-Heathrow arrived with engine spares for a stranded Tu-104 that was operating the once-weekly Aeroflot flight from Leningrad to London. CCCP-11031 is seen near the back of the BEA hangars in the winter sun of November 1967. The aircraft crashed on take-off from Kammeniy Cape in October 1970.

Ghana, formerly known as the British African Territory of the Gold Coast became independent in 1957. The newly-formed Ghana Airways, under the direction of President Nkrumah, signed a deal with the Soviet Union that included the purchase of eight Il-18s and one An-12 freighter. The sole An-12 was delivered to Ghana Airways in October 1961 as 9G-AAZ. This aircraft was rarely seen in the western world and was short-lived with the airline. Unfortunately, it was withdrawn from use during 1962 and returned to the Soviet Union during 1963. After thirty-five years, the aircraft with a confirmed construction number of 024009, built at Voronezh, has still not been reported and to this day its fate remains unknown.
(*Dr Jean Magendie Collection.*)

The little radial engine An-14 Pchelka (Little Bee) was a rare aircraft to find in its operational heyday. The nine-seater predecessor of the An-28 of which approximately 330 were built was delivered to Aeroflot and TABSO as a feeder liner and to the Soviet and East German Air Forces as a general-purpose liaison aircraft. Two other examples went to Yugoslavia and Mongolia. The subject of our picture is one of seven aircraft originally delivered to TABSO, transferred to Balkan and then transferred to the Bulgarian Government fleet. It appears that each of the seven state industrial departments had one An-14 each between 1972 and 1980, by which time all seven examples were withdrawn from use and disposed of. Furthermore, it is quite likely that Bulgaria was the last country to use the rare An-14. LZ-7001, formerly LZ-TEA, is seen parked outside the general aviation hangars at Sofia in August 1978, and operated by the Water Pollution Control Authority.

Throughout the 1960s, the Soviet Union flew the world's two largest aircraft. One was the passenger turboprop Tu-114 and the other was the An-22 freighter. This giant freighter was capable of carrying 80,000 kilograms. Fortunately, the An-22 was able to be seen up to 1989 as a regular visitor to the Paris Air Show. At the time of writing, the An-22 has been around for thirty years with many examples having been withdrawn from use, however, several examples continue to fly with the Soviet military albeit looking in poor condition. The role of the An-22 has been taken over by the versatile Il-76 and An-124 freighters. CCCP-09349 is pictured at Paris-Le Bourget in June 1973; four years later this actual aircraft crashed in June 1977.

Above:
Between 1969 and 1974, CAAC took delivery of forty-two Antonov An-24s for inter-provincial routes. Most of these examples have been broken up after retirement, relegated to ground trainers for engineering apprentices, fire trainers or transferred to China United Airlines. Since the introduction of the Chinese-built Y-7 in 1984, the CAAC policy states that all An-24s registered in China be replaced by the locally manufactured Y-7 which has now been completed. Up to 1984 the CAAC An-24s carried the original three-figure registrations. Very few of the original An-24s were ever photographed; however, B-472 is seen here on the ramp at Guangzhou-Baiyan Airport in October 1980 awaiting its next turn of duty back into the Chinese interior.

Above:
Mongolian Airlines is one of those rare airlines that most civil aircraft enthusiasts only dream of. Several of the early An-24Bs are still flying in the 1990s and believe me, they are old! The author had the pleasure of flying in bHMAY-10103. On boarding this lightly-loaded airliner there was great difficulty in finding a seat with a seat-belt, however, when one was found it was devoid of buckles and had to be tied in a granny knot! Our illustration shows bHMAY-9807 at Saynshand in southern Mongolia way back in September 1978. It is interesting to see behind the nose area of the aircraft, the traditional Mongolian residence called a *Yurt*.

Another long-serving Soviet-built airliner is the Antonov An-24, very similar in design to the Fokker Friendship. The An-24 first flew in December 1959 and after the usual Aeroflot trials entered service with Aeroflot in October 1962. Production was established at three plants; Ulan Ude and Irkutsk produced about four hundred examples between them, and Kiev built the remainder, totalling around one thousand. These neat little forty-eight-seat turboprops were widely sold around the world to socialist countries and are still very much in evidence after thirty-six years of flying.

Our first An-24 photograph is the demonstrator at the 1969 Paris Air Show. This actual aircraft was also present at the 1967 show carrying the show number of 234. Two years later it was displayed as exhibit 831. CCCP-46280 was originally built at Kiev as a standard passenger version and later converted to an An-24RT freighter/combi. Regrettably this smart-looking example crashed short of the runway at Kursk in March 1981 and was subsequently destroyed.

Any picture of the original An-24s in Aeroflot's first colours are regarded as rare. CCCP-47259 in its original form, is one such example seen at Berlin-Schönefeld in August 1972. At the time, the aircraft was less than one-year-old and flew in from Minsk on a schedule service. CCCP-47259 appears to have spent its life at Minsk and is still an active member of the Belavia fleet which is based at Minsk.

The Balkan An-24 flagship LZ-ANA after its repaint into Balkan's first red colour. The aircraft is seen on the ramp at Varna in 1972, three years before it crashed after take-off from Sofia in November 1975.

CCCP-46211, an Antonov An-24B, unusually devoid of Aeroflot titles was one of the few An-24s operated by Aeroflot's Polar Division-Special Tasks Research. The aircraft flew in from Moscow-Sheremetyevo Airport to collect a group of East German scientists who were being transported far into the Soviet Arctic for research studies. The aircraft wears an unusual version of the polar colours and displays an attractive polar emblem of the white polar bear on each side of the fuselage. This rare example was photographed at Berlin-Schönefeld Airport on a cold and bright morning in October 1976, parked outside the original terminal building. CCCP-46211 was built in 1966 and thirty years later is still flying for Aeroflot from Moscow-Bykovo Airport.

16

CCCP-46296 is one of nearly a thousand An-24s operated by Aeroflot in its post-1975 colours and photographed outside the original terminal building at Berlin-Schönefeld in June 1978. This particular aircraft, although in Aeroflot's standard colours, is a special calibration aircraft packed with instrumentation for civil and military use. The aircraft has not been recorded since 1980 and one can assume that it is lying derelict somewhere in the former Soviet Union.

The seven Antonov An-24s of Interflug took up their position at Berlin-Schönefeld Airport in 1965 to operate domestic routes within East Germany to Erfurt, Leipzig and Dresden. During the early part of 1974 all seven An-24s were withdrawn from use, stored for some considerable time and eventually in 1976 six of the fleet were sold to Hang Khong Vietnam and DM-SBH went to Balkan. Although rarely photographed, we see DM-SBH cruising along the inner taxyway on its long journey to the end of Berlin-Schönefeld's runway in August 1972.

Since 1966 TABSO, Bulgarian Air Transport and Balkan have operated sixteen An-24s some of which are still current. The first Bulgarian civil An-24 was LZ-ANA, originally delivered to TABSO in 1966 in their blue colours. The An-24s were used for domestic services and short-range international routes to the neighbouring Balkan countries. One of the few examples photographed is the flagship of the fleet, LZ-ANA, seen at Zürich-Kloten Airport in May 1967 in its full TABSO colours with Bulgarian Air Transport titles.

The flight operations of Misrair and Egyptair using An-24s can only be described as a horror story. Ten An-24s were originally delivered to Misrair in 1965. In February 1966, SU-AOB crashed during a test flight from Luxor. The following month of March 1966, SU-AOA slammed into the sand-dunes whilst approaching Cairo. A few days later, SU-AOM made aviation history; on an early morning flight from Luxor the aircraft was taking off and struck a wandering camel on the runway. Panel damage was incurred and later the same day after temporary repairs the aircraft took off for Cairo and crashed on landing, being damaged beyond repair. SU-AOM is probably the only airliner in the world to be pranged twice in one day. SU-AOL was the next casualty in August 1968, when it dived into the Mediterranean Sea near Port Said. Next to be pranged was SU-AOK, performing an undercarriage collapse at Luxor in January 1970. This performance was closely followed in March 1970, by SU-AOC, repeating Oscar Kilo's wheels-up landing, however, Oscar Charlie was supported by an engine explosion that caused the wheels-up landing. Finally, SU-ANZ stalled after take-off from Cairo in July 1970.

Three survivors from the fleet of ten were bravely incorporated into Egyptair's fleet and surprisingly survived until their withdrawal from service in 1974. The survivors, SU-ANV, SU-ANX and SU-ANY, were parked at Cairo until the 1980s. They eventually disappeared, their fate unknown. SU-AOL visited London-Heathrow Airport in October 1967 together with SU-AOC. Ten months after this picture was shot on Heathrow's 'north side', the aircraft crashed into the Mediterranean Sea on a flight from Cairo to Damascus. All forty passengers went down with the aircraft.

SP-LTH in its original form was one of twenty An-24s operated by Polskie Linie Lotnicze. The fleet was confined to domestic routes within Poland and rarely ventured outside the country. SP-LTH was substituting for an Il-18 when it made a surprise visit to London-Heathrow Airport in April 1967. This actual aircraft, originally named *Brda* survived to be repainted into LOT's current colours and in 1991 was sold to Air Ukraine as UR-49250.

This rare shot shows one of the three Egyptair survivors, SU-ANY, at Luxor in April 1973. The An-24s operated many tourists' flights from Cairo to Luxor and Aswân to see the massive dam that was built to control the mighty River Nile.

Right:
Mali, land-locked in west Africa, became independent in October 1960, thus breaking almost one hundred years of French-influence rule. Under its new independent leader Modibo Kieta, the newly formed airline of Air Mali turned to the Soviet Union for low-cost airliners. The An-2, An-24, Il-14 and Il-18 aircraft were soon delivered to their capital airport at Bamako. Two An-24s were delivered to Air Mali in 1968 and before a camera could be aimed at TZ-ACK, it was returned to the Soviet Union in 1972. TZ-ACT soldiered on alone until it crashed on take-off from downtown Timbuktu. The aircraft suffered engine failure and exploded. Forty-eight passengers and four crew perished. In this rare shot, TZ-ACT is being prepared for a flight from Bamako in April 1972.

Below:
Since 1965, Tarom has purchased forty An-24s for domestic routes within Romania and short-range international routes to neighbouring eastern European countries. Several examples have ventured into western Europe, however, in the 1990s the Tarom An-24s are now classified as vintage. All of the An-24RTs and most of the An-24Bs have been retired and broken up for scrap and a known six examples have been lost in accidents and four sold to Russia. In 1996 fifteen An-24s still remained with Tarom all of which are An-24RVs with short futures. YR-AME was withdrawn from use in 1989 and stored at Bucharest pending purchase by Aeroflot which eventually happened. The aircraft is now RA-49287 with Cheremshanka Airlines of Krasnoyarsk and now operates alongside four other members of the old Tarom fleet. Our picture shows an early example, YR-AME, seen at Bucharest in September 1975 keeping company with the last of the Tarom Il-14s.

Vietnam's An-24 fleet came complete from Interflug in 1976 except for two machines. One such example was the Vietnam Government's An-24, VN1094, later being incorporated into the Hang Khong Vietnam fleet as VN-B234. Some time during 1990, the aircraft was one of a few which sported the new company image of Vietnam Airlines. Seen as an active airliner, VN-B234 awaits its next turn of duty at Ho Chi Minh (Saigon). This aircraft is still rotting away in the sub-tropical humidity of Southern Vietnam.

Many An-24s have found their way into Air Force fleets as VIP transports. One such rare VIP transport was 030 of the Bulgarian Air Force, photographed from the 'viewing area' at Prague-Ruzyne on a bitterly cold day in January 1978. During the 1970s this aircraft was difficult to find and even more difficult to photograph; however, since the East-West barriers have fallen this aircraft can easily be found intact at Vrazhdebna, the Bulgarian Air Force transport base.

Other extremely rare VIP An-24s were the four examples operated by the Polish Air Force and later transferred to LOT. 015 visited Stockholm in 1971 where it was photographed, and during October 1974 was transferred to LOT as SP-LTU, lasting until March 1981 when it crashed on approach to Simpole, the cause being propeller failure.

The early An-26, primarily the military and cargo version of the An-24, also fits into the vintage category. The first examples were manufactured in 1969 and approximately 1,300 examples rolled off the Kiev-Svyetoshino production line.

CCCP-83966, operated by the Antonov Design Bureau as one of the company demonstrators, is depicted at Prague-Ruzyne in May 1973 on its way to the Paris Air Show. After the 1973 show and its return to the Soviet Union, the aircraft was converted to an An-32 prototype and demonstrator for the Bureau.

The eight An-24s of the Sudan Air Force are from the small production line at Irkutsk, all manufactured around 1968. Twenty years later the fleet was withdrawn from use and stored. Our picture shows an active and serviceable 911 at Khartoum in 1978.

No book relating to Soviet-built aircraft would be complete without featuring an example from the Soviet Air Force. Many An-26s are still operational, however, their appearance is rather shabby. 03 is seen in pristine condition at Pardubice, Czechoslovakia in June 1981. 03 was acting as a support aircraft for a regular regiment exchange with the Czechoslovakian Air Force.

The aerial surveyor and cargo combi of the Antonov family is the An-30, based on the well-proven airframe of the An-24. Approximately 150 were built and about twenty were exported. An early example is CCCP-46634 with a blue rudder, seen here at Berlin-Schönefeld in August 1978. The aircraft is still flying as RA-46634 with Myachkovo Air Services.

As previously stated, CCCP-83966 as an
An-26 was possibly converted to the
prototype An-32. The aircraft, owned by
the Antonov Design Bureau, displays its
Aeroflot colours as a demonstrator at the
Paris Air Show in June 1977.
(*Christian Volpati.*)

The Ilyushin Il-14 first flew in March 1953 and entered Aeroflot service in November 1954 as an Il-14P (18-seat version) followed by the Il-14M (modified 24–32-seat version). In the Soviet Union two production lines existed; the first was factory GAZ-34 at Tashkent which produced about 350 Il-14Ps between 1954 and 1957; the second being factory GAZ-30 at Khodinka which produced around a thousand Il-14Ps and Il-14Ms between 1956 and 1958. Outside the Soviet Union, Czechoslovakia produced two hundred Avia-14s at Letnany between 1956 and 1960. In neighbouring East Germany, the VEB factory at Dresden produced eighty examples as the VEB-14 between 1956 and

1958. The total production of the Il-14 was around 1,650 examples of all versions.

In previous years the Il-14 was thought to have been produced in large numbers exceeding 3,000 examples leading to the aircraft being compared with the DC-3, however, a more accurate comparison can be made with the Convair 240/340/440 series and the Martin 202/204 airliners in terms of shape, performance, production and time period. The Il-14 is no doubt a Russian classic airliner and fortunately many examples have been preserved or displayed as museum exhibits. Very few were photographed in their illustrious days as front-line airliners, especially in colour. The next few pages show the rugged radial

engined Il-14s in their former glory.

CAAC needed forty Il-14s for their fleet to operate local international flights to neighbouring countries and major provincial and regional flights within China. The Il-14 fleet of CAAC came from all four production lines during the late 1950s and were finally retired in the mid-1980s. 612 of CAAC is a real vintage gem, being built at Tashkent in 1955 and delivered straight to China. The aircraft is seen at Guangzhou in company with a CAAC Viscount in December 1980, still wearing its original aerial strake along the length of the roof.

CCCP-91611 being an Il-14M is seen parked at Leningrad-Pulkovo Airport in August 1978. By this time the aircraft had finished its useful life as a passenger airliner and was operated by one of Aeroflot's many research institutes.

Another rare colour shot from Berlin is VEB-14 DM-SAK. This example displays its intermediate colours of Deutsche Lufthansa blue and Interflug titles during the transition period of 1963, when it was photographed standing outside the old terminal building at Berlin-Schönefeld Airport. DM-SAK was delivered to Deutsche Lufthansa in October 1958 and withdrawn from Interflug service in October 1965. Early in 1966 it was sold to the Syrian Air Force.

Originally all East German Air Force VEB-14s were finished in overall bare metal silver and one such example is seen at Berlin-Schönefeld Airport in 1970. 421 spent its life with the East German Air Force as a general transport aircraft for personnel. With so many jet transports infiltrating the EGAF, it was no surprise when 421 was struck off charge in 1980 and subsequently broken up.

DM-SAH joined Deutsche Lufthansa as new from the VEB factory at Dresden in December 1957. Looking resplendent in its Interflug colours, the aircraft is parked at Berlin-Schönefeld Airport shortly before its withdrawal in 1965. DM-SAH was then moved to Dessau Zoo for display and lasted until 1988 when it was broken up for scrap.

In full camouflage colours, 485 runs up its radial engines in preparation for departure from Berlin-Schönefeld in August 1978. This magnificent-looking VEB-14 at the time was just about due for retirement and by 1980 was reduced to scrap.

After the 1956 Hungarian uprising, Malév were left with a small and battered fleet of Li-2s as their front-line airliner. The Soviet Union and East Germany obligingly supplied Malév with a fleet of eight Il-14s for passenger work. A further two examples were supplied, HA-MAG and HA-VLG, the latter being re-registered HA-MAK. The Malév Il-14s were delivered between 1957 and 1958 to provide European services until their withdrawal in 1970. All ten Il-14s were initially painted in Malév's early colours with a blue flash on the tail. By 1960 the fleet colours were changed to large Malév titles and an artistic letter M on the tail, the same as the early Il-18s. HA-MAE an East German-built VEB-14 waits at Paris-Le Bourget Airport for its patrons' return flight to Budapest in March 1964. This actual aircraft was converted to a freighter in 1966 and withdrawn from use in 1970 when it was sold to the Soviet Union.

A classic scene on the ramp at Vienna in August 1967. HA-MAI with engines still running prepares to park after its short flight from Budapest. The ground engineer is seen dragging a large pair of chocks to secure the aircraft during its two-hour turnaround. The LOT Il-18 in the background, carefully watched by a ground engineer, goes through the stages of starting all four turboprop engines ready for its flight to Warsaw. To the right of the Il-18 is a Qantas V-Jet Boeing 707. The photograph shows three generations of passenger airliners.

An old Tashkent Il-14 of 1956 vintage. Originally delivered as HA-VLG to the Hungarian Government, this aircraft was then transferred to Malév as HA-MAK. One year later in 1961, the aircraft was transferred to the Hungarian Air Force as 102 in a VIP Configuration. 102 is parked at Berlin-Schönefeld in July 1972 on one of its many military visits. During the mid-1970s it was sold back to the Soviet Union and never reported again.

TABSO–Bulgarian Air Transport took delivery of eight Il-14s in 1956 for international routes from Sofia. Some time around 1969, the airline changed its identity to Balkan and adopted a new colour image.

Here, LZ-ILC, an East German-built VEB-14, trundles along the taxyway at Frankfurt in 1964 in its full TABSO colours. This actual aircraft survived to the end of Balkan's Il-14 operations in 1974 and was subsequently broken up for scrap at Kjustendil.

Left:
The Bulgarian Air Force operated nine Il-14s as a mixture of VIP, cargo and general troop transporters. 82 was one of the rare Il-14G cargo versions that worked late into its life until 1979. The aircraft is parked on the ramp at Berlin-Schönefeld in August 1978 clearly displaying its large cargo door. After its retirement from active service, 82 was despatched to Bozuriste and displayed in the town.

Above:
The Bulgarian Il-14s in their Balkan red colours flew for about five years until their retirement in 1974. LZ-ILD, an East German-built VEB-14 is seen parked at Varna in August 1972. It is interesting to see that most passenger airliners have their main boarding door on the port side. All versions of the Il-14 had their door on the starboard side.

Opposite Below:
The first six CSA Avıa-14s, OK-LCA–LCF, all survived to the end of Czech Airlines' piston-engined era. The flagship OK-LCA and its sister aircraft OK-LCB were converted to pure freighters during 1966. Both aircraft originally wore a bare-metal scheme and later were painted in CSA's normal red colours. In this rare shot OK-LCB is seen in its bare-metal scheme at Prague-Ruzyne Airport in May 1968. On the port side of the aircraft a large cargo door is fitted. Both freighters were withdrawn from use during March 1977 and immediately sold to the Soviet Union.

Above:
CSA operated an all Czechoslovakian-built Avia-14 fleet of thirty-four airliners from 1957 to 1977. Initially many of the fleet were used on international routes until the arrival of the Il-18 and Tu-104, then becoming the backbone of the airline's domestic routes. The entire fleet was delivered to CSA in their original blue colours that lasted until 1960 when all the Avia-14s were repainted in the more familiar red colours.

OK-MCP, less than two years old, is depicted in the original Ceskoslovenské Aerolinie blue colours leaving Paris-Le Bourget in 1959. OK-MCP was one of the many December 1974 withdrawals from service and joined the mass purchase of Avia-14s by the Soviet Union.
(*Tom Singfield Collection.*)

OK-LCE upon its early retirement from the CSA fleet in 1966 was transferred to the CSSDL Calibration fleet. It is seen outside the Prague-Ruzyne government hangars, in company with a locally made Skoda estate car in 1974. OK-LCE was replaced by a Yak-40 in 1977 and also joined the bulk sale of Avia-14s to the Soviet Union.

In this extremely rare shot inside the maintenance hangar at Prague-Ruzyne, OK-MCX is receiving attention in April 1974. Less than one year later, OK-MCX was also on its way to the Soviet Union.

A portrait of a classic . . . OK-MCU complete with its oil-stained engine nacelles, rests between duties in the summer of August 1973 at Prague-Ruzyne.

Opposite Above:
At least fifty-seven Avia-14s were operated by the Czechoslovakian Air Force from 1957 to around the late 1970s. Most of the large fleet were finished in bare metal with a registration and air force roundel. A very small number were classed as VIP versions. One such VIP example was 3154 seen here at Prague-Ruzyne in August 1976 and definitely in need of a paint-job. It is interesting to see this aircraft with tip tanks which very few military examples had. The fate of this shabby-looking classic has never been established.

Opposite Below:
The original LSFMV Government air fleet was founded in 1946 and all aircraft of this fleet were registered OK-BYA to OK-BYZ. Many of these registrations have been used several times on different types of airliners over a period of fifty years. Five Avia-14s operated with the LSFMV from 1957 and 1975. The fleet was not as frequently used as the CSA fleet and when the Government replaced the Avia-14s, four went to CSA and the fifth one went to the Air Force.

OK-BYU was a standard Avia-14 with an eighteen-seat interior and was unusually fitted with tip tanks, normally associated with the Super Avia-14-32. This rare example paid a visit to London-Heathrow on a dismal day in April 1966. Later in 1975, OK-BYU was transferred to CSA for two years as OK-MCD and devoid of tip tanks.

Above:
The fleet of LOT Il-14s were somewhat more rare than those of other eastern European operators of this type. During the late-1950s when the twenty-three examples were being delivered, LOT operated a fleet of five Convair 340s and three Viscounts and preference, probably for political purposes, was given to these western types on western routes, hence the small number of LOT Il-14s that flew outside Poland.

SP-LNE, a 1956 Tashkent-built Il-14P in its original LOT colours is being prepared for its return flight to Warsaw from Paris-Le Bourget in July 1959. SP-LNE was cancelled from the LOT fleet in 1974 and transferred to Aeropol who used the aircraft for ad hoc charter work and later for aerial surveys. It was eventually retired from Aeropol and has been reported as discarded at Warsaw as late as 1993. (*Tom Singfield Collection.*)

SP-LNH is shown in its final Il-14 colours with LOT. Lima November Hotel was an East German-built VEB-14 rarely seen in the West, however, on this occasion the aircraft is seen approaching the ramp area at Geneva in June 1966. SP-LNH was withdrawn from use in 1971 and sold to the Soviet Union in 1972.

TZ-ABH is one of three very rare Il-14s operated by Air Mali. During the early 1960s these three examples were rarely seen outside of the west African area as they only operated to their neighbouring countries. TZ-ABH is seen at Marseille in June 1964 whilst on its way back to the Soviet Union for heavy maintenance. Just over one year later in September 1965, TZ-ABH came to grief and crashed at Col de la Cayolle, France. The aircraft was totally destroyed. The fate of the two remaining Il-14s of Air Mali has never been established.

Tarom's fleet of twenty Il-14s consisting of eleven Russian-built and nine East German-built were delivered in 1956, initially for local international routes and later relegated to domestic routes until their final retirement in 1977. Most of the fleet were sold to the Soviet Union in 1978.

In this rare colour shot, YR-ILE a Soviet-built Il-14P complete with original shallow roof fin and bearing Tarom's old colours, awaits its passengers at Athens in March 1962.

Above:
YR-ILO, an East German-built VEB-14 in the later colours of Tarom is seen on the ramp at Vienna in August 1967. Regrettably this fine-looking airliner was destroyed in an accident at Sibiu, Romania in March 1976.

Left:
Air Guinee were given six Avia-14s with financial assistance from the Soviet Union in 1960. One such rare example was 3X-GAH, originally 1109 with the Czechoslovakian Air Force, being prepared for a flight from Dakar in March 1965. The fate of this aircraft remains unknown.

In 1957 during the decade of 'Soviet aviation gifts', the Nepalese Government were presented with an Il-14 and An-2 for use by the Nepalese Royal Flight. The reigning monarch, King Mahendra B.B. Shah and his royal family used both luxuriously-fitted aircraft until their retirement in 1970. 9N-RF1 a Khodinka-built Il-14M is seen stored between royal duties at Kathmandu in November 1968 in this magnificent Himalayan hide-away. (*Tom Singfield Collection.*)

The 1950s saw a generation of heavy turboprop airliners produced in the western world, the Britannia, Vanguard and Electra being the recognisable types. In the Soviet Union the elegant Ilyushin Il-18 was the answer to this wonderful era of heavy propliners. The prototype Il-18 first flew in 1957 and after manufacturing 569 examples the last Il-18 rolled off the Khodinka production line in 1969,

effectively marking the end of the world's heavy propliner production. Approximately 430 Il-18s were operated by Aeroflot from 1959 until their final replacement by the Tu-154 around 1984. A small number of Il-18s still fly within Russia, however, they are rapidly disappearing.

A classic and nostalgic shot from the roof gardens above Terminal Two at London-Heathrow in April 1964. CCCP-75816 waits

for its trade delegation to board, whilst in the background CCCP-75823 taxies between the Il-18 and a parked BEA Vanguard. The fate of CCCP-75816 has never been established, however, CCCP-75823 was damaged beyond repair in a hard landing at Yuzhno-Sakhalinsk in the Soviet Far East way back in August 1970.

A magnificent portrait of B-216 in active service for CAAC. Inbound from Chengdu, B-216 has cut its outboard engines and is preparing to turn into gate 2 at Beijing Capital Airport. The sight and sound of a CAAC Il-18 disappeared very quickly after the crash of B-222 at Chongqing in 1988.

This shot can only be described as a 'Gatwick Classic'. Amidst the pomp and ceremony at London-Gatwick in February 1967, an immaculate-looking CCCP-75412 is being prepared for departure after the visit of Leonid Brezhnev and other Soviet officials. As you can see, security wasn't a problem in 1967!

After Fidel Castro seized power in 1959, Cuba became isolated from the western world and turned to the Soviet Union for every need, including aircraft. Vast numbers of Soviet-built aircraft appeared on the Cuban register including five Il-18s all of which were delivered in their original colours of Cubana de Aviacion.

The first of the five Il-18s was CU-T830 and undoubtedly the rare bird of the fleet. Delivered in 1964, the aircraft crashed within two years at Cienfuegos, Cuba in July 1966 and was totally destroyed. In this rare picture CU-T830 is seen at Mexico City in company with Aeromexico and Mexicana DC-6s in October 1965.

54

Whilst waiting for deliveries of the
Tu-154Ms in 1985, CAAC leased three
Il-18s from Tarom for passenger operations
by the Northwest Division based in Xian.
This extremely rare example of B-232 is
shown being prepared for a flight from the
old Xian Airport close to the Xian city
centre. The original airport has long since
gone, being demolished as part of the ring
road improvements.

Above:

During the transition period from Deutsche Lufthansa to Interflug in 1963 a few Il-18s carried their old Deutsche Lufthansa colours and Interflug titles making these airliners extremely rare. One such example was DM-STG parked at Berlin-Schönefeld as late as May 1964 in the dual markings.

Malév of Hungary have had an unhappy association with Soviet-built airliners and the Il-18 was no exception, losing four aircraft in fatal accidents. HA-MOC was one such fatality. Delivered in 1961, Mike Oscar Charlie was seven miles out on approach to Copenhagen in bad weather in August 1971, when it had to ditch into the sea. The aircraft took all forty-two passengers and crew to the bottom of the Baltic Sea. In better times, HA-MOC departs from London-Gatwick passing a Lloyd International DC-4 in August 1966.

Opposite Below:
DM-STL was one of fourteen Il-18s that flew for Interflug for twenty-nine years. The only Interflug Il-18 fatality was DM-STL; the aircraft was operating a cargo flight in south-west Africa when it crashed after take-off in March 1979 from Luanda, Angola. The aircraft was totally destroyed. As a pure long-range Il-18D passenger airliner, DM-STL is seen as such at Berlin-Schönefeld in August 1972.

Above:
Seen at Berlin-Schönefeld in August 1972, Bulgarian Il-18 LZ-BEP wears the TABSO-Balkan red colours with Cyrillic script titles. Bravo Echo Papa became the fifth Bulgarian Il-18 casualty when at Sana in June 1984 it overran the runway after a late touchdown and had no chance of stopping until arrested by the boundary fence and other airport equipment; however, all occupants survived the rather unorthodox landing. Regrettably the aircraft was severely damaged beyond repair and scrapped on site.

Opposite Above:
At the time of writing, Bulgaria has operated twenty-one Il-18s since 1962, displaying four different company liveries and five examples have been lost in accidents. LZ-BEV in TABSO blue colours and Bulgarian Air Transport titles taxies away from its gate at London-Gatwick after push-back in June 1967. LZ-BEV was retired from Balkan and subsequently moved to a playground park in Sofia, where in 1992 it was severely damaged by fire.

Opposite Below:
Another classic Gatwick shot . . . this time LZ-BEK of Bulair in June 1969 operating a Bulgarian holiday charter. LZ-BEK was later transferred to the Balkan fleet in 1972 and lasted the distance until its retirement in 1984. It was stored at Varna for several months and broken up for useful spares and scrapped during 1985.

North Korean Il-18s have always been rare and P-835 and P-836 have always been the two examples reported at Berlin-Schönefeld and Prague-Ruzyne. A third example, 825 has also been reported at Berlin-Schönefeld, however, the really rare Il-18 is 525 and is seen here taxying into the ramp area after landing at Berlin-Schönefeld in June 1970.

Opposite Above:
OK-NAB, still with its roof fin, is preparing for take-off from Copenhagen in February 1968. Alpha Bravo was one of three CSA Il-18 casualities. The aircraft overshot the runway at Bratislava and turned right too sharply. The immediate result was that Alpha Bravo nose-dived into a lake and all seventy-six onboard were killed.

Opposite Below:
Probably the most common of all Il-18s were the Polish LOT fleet. The ten examples all survived nearly thirty years with LOT and although they may have nearly sent LOT bankrupt, at least they gave reliable service. SP-LSB was delivered to LOT in April 1961 and retired in January 1990. Regrettably this beautiful-looking airliner was broken up for scrap in February 1990 at Warsaw. Looking in pristine condition, Lima Sierra Bravo taxies into the ramp area at Paris-Le Bourget in August 1968 passing a new Aer Lingus BAC One-Eleven.

The Polish Air Force have operated five different Il-18s spanning twenty years and oddly enough only two registrations have been used, 101 and 102. Our picture shows the second 102 in its full glory parked on London-Heathrow's south side in April 1969.

As previously mentioned, Misrair, United Arab Airlines and Egyptair flight operations with the An-24 were a sad disaster. The situation continued with the Il-18s and one had to be quick off the mark to photograph these airliners before they became a pile of wreckage. United Arab Airlines took delivery of four Il-18s. SU-AOV and SU-AOX survived to be integrated into the new Egyptair fleet; SU-AOY also got as far as Egyptair but in January 1973 it slammed into the Kyrenian mountains whilst on approach to Nicosia taking all thirty-seven passengers and crew with it. SU-APC, delivered to United Arab Airlines in March 1969, only lasted two weeks when on its third approach to Aswân it crashed one thousand metres short of the runway. The aircraft was totally destroyed, as were its one hundred unlucky occupants.

SU-AOY in full United Arab Airlines colours during one of its rare visits to London-Heathrow is seen parked next to a BKS Britannia in March 1970. Three years later SU-AOY became another Egyptian Il-18 statistic.

At the end of the Vietnam War, the Soviet Union gave Vietnam several transport airliners to form the base of a new national airline, namely Hang Khong Vietnam. Three Il-18s took up their position with the state transport authority and VN-195 when it first appeared operated as a VIP transport for the new North Vietnam Government. In 1976 the aircraft was re-registered as VN-B195 and carried the senior Vietnamese Government officials to Europe visiting Helsinki and Paris where at Paris-Orly the aircraft is seen parked in April 1977 as the sun sets low on a spring evening.

Opposite Above:
The second Egyptian Il-18 to survive Egyptair's aerial extermination was SU-AOX. The aircraft is seen in full Egyptair colours on its last visit to London-Heathrow in September 1973. Shortly after, it was retired and in 1975 was returned to the Soviet Union.

Opposite Below:
In 1965, Air Mali leased two Il-18s from Aeroflot for their local African routes and their longer routes to Cairo and Paris via Geneva. TZ-ABE in its original form with its roof fin is parked awaiting its return flight to Bamako. Regrettably TZ-ABE ended its flying days by running out of fuel whilst approaching Lingomin, Upper Volta and crashed killing all forty-seven on board. This rare and nostalgic shot was taken in July 1968 in company with the French prototype Concorde at Paris-Le Bourget.

Top:
Tarom operated fifteen Il-18s all of which were regular visitors to western Europe during the 1960s and 1970s. The flagship of the Il-18 fleet, YR-IMA in its unmodified form prepares to turn and dock at Paris-Le Bourget in July 1968, whilst passing another Il-18 classic, 3X-GAT of Air Guinee.

Above:
3X-GAX of Air Guinee looking immaculate on the parking stand at Berlin-Schönefeld in August 1978. Twelve days after this picture was shot, 3X-GAX crashed into swampy marshlands whilst approaching its base airport at Conakry.

As mentioned previously with the Ghana Airways An-12, a substantial deal was agreed with the governments of Ghana and the Soviet Union to purchase eight Il-18s between November 1960 and May 1962. As the aircraft were introduced to the Ghana Airways routes it became apparent that the Il-18 was uneconomical to operate and expensive to maintain. During 1963 the first examples were withdrawn from use and by mid-1964 the fleet of eight was grounded at Accra. By 1965 the fleet of eight had been returned to the Soviet Union and replaced by a single Bristol Britannia and an ambitious plan to purchase four Vc-10s of which only two were delivered.

Ghana Airways released some interesting details relating to the purchase of the Il-18s. Each Il-18 cost £670,000 including four spare engines. Payment was 10% deposit and the balance payable over eight years at 2.5% per annum. Owing to the low engine time between overhauls and the necessity to overhaul in the Soviet Union, the airliners soon became an economic disaster. Only 225 hours per aircraft per year was achieved and the average load factor per flight was 20%, resulting in enormous losses. Pictures of the Ghana Airways Il-18s are extremely rare especially in colour; however, depicted here is 9G-AAL on its only visit to London-Heathrow in June 1961. The aircraft is parked on the BOAC maintenance ramp where the British Airways Boeing 747 hangars now stand.

Several governments around the world used the Il-18 as a VIP transport; some were frequently seen, some were extremely rare. One such rare Il-18 was operated by the Yugoslav Air Force. Originally delivered as YU-AIA to the Yugoslav Government in 1967, the aircraft only lasted one year before being transferred to the Yugoslav Air Force as 7501. In the 1970s it was re-registered yet again as 73201 and remained as such until the early 1980s when it was retired and replaced with a Boeing 727. 73201 is seen here standing at Mangere Airport, Auckland, New Zealand in March 1973, when it carried President Tito on a state visit to New Zealand and Australia.

Many of the early Soviet-built jet airliners including the IL-62 have become museum exhibits and in the 1990s, enthusiasts are hard-pressed to find any basic Il-62s still flying for passenger revenue. The Il-62 prototype first flew in 1963 and entered passenger service in 1967, effectively replacing the Tu-114s on long-haul international routes to Cuba, West Africa and India. The new Il-62s, in the late 1960s and early 1970s were frequent visitors to western Europe with a continuous flow of newly registered airliners flying into London and Paris, this trend with the Il-62 continued through to the early 1980s. By 1974 very few Il-62s in their original colours existed.

A rare vintage shot of CCCP-86662 at Paris-Le Bourget in August 1969 in pristine condition. This Aeroflot Il-62 has its registration applied to the polished engine cowlings and a small Aeroflot insignia on the tail and cockpit.

CCCP-86654 approaches Berlin-Schönefeld
in August 1972.

Regrettably CCCP-86671 became an early casualty when in October 1972 it crashed on approach to Moscow-Sheremetyevo. The aircraft was totally destroyed and all 174 onboard were killed. The aircraft is seen at London-Heathrow in June 1972, four months before that horrific crash.

CCCP-86676 was one of the last Aeroflot
Il-62s to wear its original colours and is
seen touching down complete with smoke
effects on runway 10R at London-
Heathrow in July 1973. The airliner was
last seen dumped and decaying at Tashkent
in 1992.

The rare Il-62 in the CSA fleet was OK-DBF. Originally delivered in September 1973, the aircraft only lasted twenty-three months when in August 1975, Bravo Fox came in too low on approach to Damascus. The aircraft hit a sand-dune and exploded killing all 126 onboard. Again on the end of runway 28L at London-Heathrow in November 1973, OK-DBF prepares to depart to Prague.

Poland, like Czechoslovakia were long-time users of the Il-62. LOT operated seventeen examples, only the first six basic Il-62s carried the original colours and all were returned to the Soviet Union in the early 1990s. LOT lost two Il-62s and one such fatality was SP-LAA which was returning to Warsaw from New York in March 1980. The aircraft developed an engine failure that resulted in damage to the other three engines and controls in the tail section. It crashed, powerless, a thousand metres short of the Warsaw runway and all eighty-seven onboard perished. SP-LAA is seen in better days in its original colours and proudly named *Mikolaj Kopernik*, whilst approaching London-Heathrow in August 1974.

Many readers of *Vintage Russian* will remember the Czechoslovakian political reforms and subsequent Soviet invasion of the country in April 1968. Had Alexander Dubcek had his way, CSA would probably have operated a fleet of Vc-10s, as serious talks took place between Vickers Aircraft and CSA in 1967. The Dubcek Government was forced into buying the Il-62 and initially six Aeroflot Il-62s with CSA Ceskoslovenské Aerolinie titles were leased from April 1968 to December 1969, when by that time the first two CSA Il-62s were delivered. In the soft summer sun of August 1968, CCCP-86666 is lining up for take-off from runway 28L at London-Heathrow.

During 1966, Aeroflot and Japan Airlines entered into a route-share agreement that offered passengers non-stop flights between Moscow and Tokyo. The sector was operated by two Tu-114s until mid-1969 when they were replaced with two Il-62s. CCCP-86682 in Aeroflot's old colours and complete with its Japan Airlines titles is seen parked at Brussels in October 1969.

Above:
Aeroflot leased eight Il-62s to United Arab Airlines and Egyptair between June 1971 and July 1973. The first examples, SU-ARN and SU-ARO, were Egyptian-registered with United Arab Airlines titles and flew between Cairo, Zürich and London. SU-ARO is about to push-back in the summer sun of July 1971 at London-Heathrow.

Below:
During the United Arab Airlines lease of Aeroflot Il-62s the airline changed its name due to the massive political problems in the Middle East region. Egypt's national airline then became known as Egyptair and rotating Aeroflot Il-62s then carried the Egyptair titles, registration and flag. The fifth aircraft to be leased was SU-AVU and is caught by the camera approaching Runway 28L at London-Heathrow in March 1973.

Aeroflot's strong relationship with Cuba goes back to the early 1960s when Khrushchev and Kennedy clashed over military hardware being shipped to the Cuban Island, situated on the doorstep of the United States. It was not until the introduction of the Il-62 in 1967 that Cubana titles appeared on Aeroflot airliners. When CCCP-86681 had finished its lease with Egyptair as SU-ARW it then moved to the Moscow-Havana route for twelve months and became a regular at Madrid on its refuelling stop across the mid-Atlantic. The aircraft is pushing back at Madrid in July 1973.

Above:
During the 'Cold War' years covered in this book, Soviet-built helicopters were extremely rare, difficult to access and apart from the Paris Air Show visitors, were almost impossible to photograph. Probably the rarest type to find and photograph was the little Kamov Ka-26, a multi-purpose, quick convertible twin-engined helicopter. This interesting helicopter had two piston radial engines powering a contra-rotating shaft of two sets of three-bladed rotor blades made of fibreglass. The noise generated from these motors could be heard many miles away. Aeroflot operated an estimated two hundred Ka-26s for specialised crop spraying, air ambulance and amongst other functions the highly publicised use of the Ka-26 for controlling Moscow's road traffic problems in the 1970s.

After the 1975 Paris Air Show, CCCP-26184 flew to the Battersea helipad and gave a few demonstration flights on how to control London's traffic! An invitation was extended to me to join the chase helicopter and witness the occasion, however, the result was a non-event. CCCP-26184 is seen over the River Thames with North London in the background.

Opposite Above:
DM-SPY is fitted as an agricultural version with a liquid hopper and spray bars.

Opposite Below:
DM-SPZ shows its versatility by displaying itself as an industrial crane. The winch is capable of lifting 150 kg.

Opposite Above:
At the same time as Interflug accepted its first Ka-26, DM-SPZ conducted short trials for the Volks Polizei to evaluate the effectiveness of patrolling the Berlin Wall. DM-SPZ in rare markings is seen at Berlin-Schönefeld as an Air Observation Post version complete with the insignia of the East German Volks Polizei.

Opposite Below:
The trials of DM-SPZ were obviously a success. DM-VPD was the first of eight Ka-26s delivered directly to the Volks Polizei. The helicopters' only purpose was to patrol the world's most sinister wall surrounding West Berlin.

The Lisunov Li-2 is a Douglas DC-3 Dakota produced under licence in the Soviet Union. Production started in 1940 at Moscow-Chimki. By October 1941 the production line was moved to Tashkent and remained there until the last Li-2 rolled off the line in 1954. An additional production line was established at Komsomolsk that produced 500 examples between 1946 and 1950. The total production of Li-2s stands at around 5,650. Fortunately several examples have been preserved throughout the world by previous operators of the type such as the Soviet Union, Czechoslovakia, Poland, Romania, Hungary and China.

Aeroflot used the Li-2 as a normal passenger airliner, cargo carrier and very many were used in the Arctic region for the Polar Division operating alongside Il-12s and Il-14s for many years. During the Li-2 years of polar operations, the aircraft were painted in a very dark green and black that became the forerunner of the red polar colours. CCCP-04214 as illustrated is a unique version operating on skis in place of the normal undercarriage.

Thirty Li-2s flew in China for CAAC from 1951 until their retirement in 1989. CAAC achieved excellent service from the Li-2 as a passenger airliner, aerial surveyor and cargo carrier. Our picture shows 323 still in its original form as a passenger airliner and still in service in 1985 at Taiyuan. Although 323 has now vanished since its retirement, eight known examples still exist in museums around China.

Above:

The Mil Design bureau was founded in 1947 under the leadership of Mikhail Mil who had made a name for himself as an autogiro and rotary wing designer and engineer. Mil's first commercial helicopter was the Mi-1 and named after the popular Russian car, the Moskvich. The first five years of production took place in the Soviet Union manufacturing for Aeroflot and the Soviet Air Force. In 1957 the production was transferred to Swidnik, Poland where it continued until 1965.

SP-SBA was demonstrated at the Paris Air Show in 1963 in the form of an air ambulance known as the Mil Mi-1S. The Polish-built version illustrated was known as the SM-1WS. The patient is laid in the capsule that is attached to the outside of the cabin and the only way to speak to the medical attendants onboard is to scream at full pitch into the communication tunnel, above the noise of a piston radial engine; the survival rate of the patients has never been established.

Since 1966 the Swidnik factory in Poland has produced well over three thousand Mi-2 helicopters mainly for Aeroflot and the former Iron Curtain countries' air forces. Many are still in evidence but the earlier examples are rotting away in scrapyards. One such early example visited England in 1978 with the company executives from Ursus Bizon, a Polish company that manufactured a range of agricultural vehicles. The visit was to try and sell tractors and combine harvesters to the English farmers. SP-SWG is seen parked at Needham Market in July 1978. A few hours after this Mi-2 was photographed I was invited to fly in it to Battersea Helipad with a stop at Stansted. The flight was interesting, especially at low level following the River Thames through London, however, I will never forget the mighty strong smell of fuel throughout the two-hour journey.

Opposite Below:
Another rare variant of the Polish-built SM-1 was the blunt nose variety of which little is known. This example is operated by Slov-Air as OK-RUV during the early 1960s.

The Soviet-built Mil Mi-4, now a real veteran of the helicopter world, first flew in 1952. It closely resembles the old Sikorsky S-55 Whirlwind. Thousands of Mi-4s were manufactured, many being exported to the Soviet allies' air forces during the start of the Cold War period. Today, it is more than likely that no flying examples exist and very few are evident around the world in the aviation museums.

Although complete and cosmetically appealing, CCCP-03586 is displayed in open storage on small concrete blocks at Ust Kamenogorsk. Colour material of Aeroflot Mi-4s is just about impossible to find, so we'll have to settle for a preserved example shot in 1993.

Left:
Deutsche Lufthansa operated six Mi-4s between 1961 and 1970. These rare helicopters were attached to the industrial division of Deutsche Lufthansa and never transferred to Interflug. When the fleet was retired, the first two examples went to the East German Army in 1967 and the remaining four went to GST (Gesellschaft fur Technik und Sport) as instructional airframes in 1968. DM-SPC of Deutsche Lufthansa is seen parked at Berlin-Schönefeld in 1966.

Below:
Apart from Aeroflot, very few airlines operated the Mi-4. One such operator was Royal Nepal Airlines who operated two examples in the Himalayan region. 9N-HAA is parked at Kathmandu in November 1968.

The Soviet Union has always been renowned for large aircraft and over the years has produced some really outsized aircraft and helicopters for specialised aerial work. Mil's Mi-6 was in its heyday the biggest helicopter in the world and even today is an awesome sight. An early example seen in the West was CCCP-06174 at the 1967 Paris Air Show. The helicopter, resplendent in its red display colours, is seen flying slowly past the camera in preparation for landing. This particular helicopter never made it back to the Soviet Union after the air show. It crashed into high ground near Marseille in August 1967 during a demonstration flight and was completely destroyed.

According to the massive amount of construction numbers that have been logged over the past thirty years on Mi-8 helicopters, it can be assumed that at least 15,000 of these robust and versatile helicopters have been built. Several thousand are still in service, though our picture coverage illustrates very early examples. The first Mi-8 to appear in the West was CCCP-11052 at the 1967 Paris Air Show. The following year in 1968, a smart-looking CCCP-11053 as illustrated appeared at the Turin Air Show, Italy sporting a rather nice two-tone blue livery and described as a Mi-8P with the large rectangular windows. This very early demonstrator of 1968 vintage has never been reported since.

The 1969 Paris Air Show Mi-6 demonstrator was another unusual version, being CCCP-69318 complete with stubby wings for better stability. This version, in its overall grey finish, was in fact a military version and stands proud on the ramp at Paris-Le Bourget in June 1969.

A rare and early example of a CAAC Mi-8 is seen in the form of 896 as a basic Mi-8. The Chinese Mi-8s were originally delivered to China during the mid-1970s in the old registration sequence making them good candidates for vintage helicopters.

Opposite Above:
Interflug took delivery of their first Mi-8 in 1967 as a replacement for the ageing Mi-4s. First to take up its position at Berlin-Schönefled was DM-SPA as a Mi-8T with the more familiar round windows. DM-SPA was re-registered as DDR-SPA in 1981 and was still a survivor when the collapse of East Germany occurred in 1989. The West German aviation authorities inherited all the Mi-8s and this example became D-HOXA. Since 1992 it has been preserved at Finow, where in its days of glory with Interflug, it probably spent many working hours.

Opposite Below:
Another Mi-8 from the Interflug fleet was DM-SPC, parked at Berlin-Schönefeld in company with DM-SPB in August 1978.

The Mi-10 was another of Mil's amazing designs available in two versions. The normal Mi-10 had short undercarriage legs as a general-purpose cargo and passenger version. The other version is the Mi-10K with long undercarriage legs as a flying crane for aerial construction for the Soviet Union's oil industry. This particular version of the Mi-10K is CCCP-04102, demonstrated its ability to carry a coach on a cargo platform at London-Gatwick in June 1967.

Mil's next ingenious design was the giant Mi-12, a helicopter that defied all the theories of flying. One may ask how this unusual-looking machine managed to get airborne, but somehow it did. Three examples were built; the prototype crashed, a second is reported as preserved near Moscow and the Paris demonstrator, CCCP-21142 survived long enough to be retired into Monino Museum. During its flying days of the early 1970s, CCCP-21142 is seen passing through Holland on its way to the 1971 Paris Air Show in company with the Tu-144, where both machines created worldwide interest.

The world's first jet airliner, the Tupolev Tu-104 first flew in June 1955 and entered Aeroflot service in September 1956. The airliner was based on a civil version of the Tu-16 jet-bomber and throughout its life actually looked like a military personnel carrier with its glazed nose. The first five prototypes were constructed from Tu-16 components at the GAZ-400 factory at the Moscow-Bykovo repair plant. A further seven examples known as Tu-104Gs were built before serious production of the Tu-104A began, with forty-five at Kharkov and sixty-five at Omsk. The ultimate

stretched version was the Tu-104B, of which ninety-seven examples were built at Kazan. Production of all models took place between 1955 and 1960. The entire Tu-104 production of all models went to Aeroflot with the exception of six Tu-104As that were purchased by Czech Airlines who operated them until 1973. Aeroflot's extensive use of the Tu-104 throughout the Soviet Union lasted until 1981 when the last few remaining were replaced by the Tu-154. Several examples have been preserved at various locations around Russia, however, in our picture coverage of

the Tu-104 it is featured as a front-line airliner in its days of glory and intrigue.

CCCP-n5445 arrives at Idlewild International Airport in July 1959 with a Soviet trade delegation. This Tu-104 was the highest registration ever noted in the old series of numbers and was later re-registered into the more familiar CCCP-42xxx series. The Eastern Air Lines DC-6 moving along the taxyway makes this into a classic and extremely rare picture of two countries' airliners which at the time were deeply embroiled in the Eisenhower years of the Cold War.

CCCP-42456, possibly the last Tu-104A to be built, was used for trials by the British Civil Aviation Authority during the summer months of 1966. This classic-looking airliner stands on London-Heathrow's south side parking ramp close to the old Pan American Airlines maintenance hangars in September 1966. The beautiful-looking BEA hangars are clearly seen behind this immaculate-looking Tu-104A.

Above:

On a wet Saturday morning at London-Gatwick in September 1971, I was just about to surrender to the weather when I saw a Tu-104 appear from the rain clouds. Sitting in the car (a green Mk1 Ford Consul) with the wipers ticking away, the Tu-104 landed with the aid of two parachutes acting as brakes on the rain-soaked runway. Unfortunately I was unable to photograph the actual landing with the chutes fully extended, however, as it turned on to the taxyway leading to the terminal area, CCCP-42487 was still dragging the two chutes. This spectacular manoeuvre often occurred with the Tu-104, especially when landing on short runways or in adverse weather condition like heavy rain or ice, to aid its braking ability.

Often reported as the last Tu-104 to be built, CCCP-42508 is seen at Berlin-Schönefeld Airport inbound from Moscow in the late afternoon sun in August 1972. I remember making a comment in my notebook that the condition and paintwork on 42508 was immaculate and had obviously recently received attention.

Opposite Below:
The rivals meet at London-Gatwick . . . The de Havilland Comet and the Tupolev Tu-104, both classic first generation jets, are seen in this nostalgic shot from the terrace of the southern finger at London-Gatwick on a bright Sunday morning in August 1972. Both the BEA Airtours Comets and the Aeroflot Tu-104s operated the package holiday flights to and from Leningrad each weekend. CCCP-42474, a Tu-104B, was one of three Tu-104s that dropped into Gatwick during that morning.

As mentioned earlier CSA Czech Airlines operated six Tu-104As from 1957 until 1973 on selected routes around east and west Europe. The Tu-104s were expensive to operate and somewhat unreliable and frequently gave way to the flight being operated by the CSA Il-18s. During the sixteen-year period three of the aircraft were involved in major accidents and the three survivors escaped the ultimate chop; OK-LDA went to Kbely Museum and both OK-LDC and OK-NDF ended their days as cafe bars at Touzim and Olomouc respectively.

OK-NDD glides along the taxyway at Zürich-Kloten Airport on its return flight to Prague in September 1969. Ten months later in June 1970, Delta Delta experienced difficulties whilst attempting its third landing at Tripoli, Libya. The aircraft crashed killing thirteen passengers.

Another CSA Tu-104 casualty was OK-MDE seen here approaching Berlin-Schönefeld Airport in August 1972. One year later in August 1973, Delta Echo was landing at Nicosia, Cyprus when it veered off the runway and crashed into a ditch. Fortunately, its dazed passengers all escaped after its mighty rough landing. However, it was the end for OK-MDE.

Above:

Thirty-six of these megalithic Tu-114 prop monsters were built for Aeroflot between 1957 and 1961 as long-range intercontinental airliners. The Tu-114 was also the world's largest turboprop airliner and in 1998 still holds that title. This amazingly powerful airliner with its contra-rotating props could chop through the air and cruise at the astoundingly high speed of 500 mph, which in turboprop terms is high. Regrettably only a few visited the western world and very few were photographed. The Tu-114s opened up the new long-haul route to Havana in 1963 and Montreal in 1966, however, these were short-lived and taken over by the new Il-62. Only three examples ever visited London-Heathrow. Several went to Paris and Brussels and the odd one or two went to Frankfurt, Zürich and Rome. Apart from the infrequent visits to the western world, most Tu-114 operations served the long-haul routes across the length of the Soviet Union from Moscow to the Soviet Far East. After the introduction of the Il-62, the Tu-114 was gradually phased out and by 1978 its life as an airliner had ended. A known five examples still exist as museum exhibits and three fuselages still lie at Moscow-Domodedovo Airport.

Probably the most 'common' Tu-114 was CCCP-76459. This aircraft was a regular at Paris and is seen passing Le Bourget's familiar old fuel depot in April 1968.

Above:
CCCP-76487 stands in the Montreal-Dorval sun in July 1967. The aircraft is operating its once-weekly flight from Moscow and awaits its passengers for the return leg of the journey. This beautiful-looking airliner has not been reported since 1972.

Opposite Below:
In October 1966 Brussels played host to CCCP-76470, seen here as it prepares to dock after its inbound flight from Moscow. After landing, the Tu-114s cut their outboard engines and used the two inboard engines as their power to taxy to the parking stand.

Above:
After operating a flight through Frankfurt in March 1967, CCCP-76459 is seen proceeding up the taxyway in preparation for take-off. There is no finer sight than an airliner of this size with contra-rotating props.

Right:
Dr Jean Magendie from France kindly loaned this slide for *Vintage Russian*. This fine shot of CCCP-45092 is taken at Vienna in June 1966 wearing a much lighter blue cheat line than CCCP-45068.

Below:
During the late 1970s, Aeroflot operated six out-of-sequence high numbered Tu-124s all being reported at Berlin, Warsaw, Prague and Sofia. One such example, CCCP-45158, is seen at Sofia as late as July 1980.

Above:
As previously stated, Aeroflot adopted a new style of colours in 1975. CCCP-45095, bearing the new colours, comes from the Tom Singfield Collection. Unfortunately, the date and location are unknown.

Below:
Interflug's second Tu-124 is somewhat of a mystery machine. According to Interflug, after the collapse of East Germany DM-SDB was transferred to the Air Force as 496 in 1974. However, during August 1974, the author witnessed all four East German Tu-124s on the ground at the same time. To further confuse the historical identity of these Tu-124s, DM-SDB is seen roaring away on take-off from Berlin-Schönefeld later the same day, clearly showing an air force-type cheat line; so what was the other mystery Tu-124 of the air force left on the ground parked behind 495 and DM-SDA?

Above:
Czech Airlines were the first of three customers outside the Soviet Union to buy the Tu-124. The three aircraft were ordered in 1964 and were overshadowed by the larger Tu-104s. OK-TEB crashed at Zürich in 1970 and OK-TEA and OK-UEC soldiered on until their retirement in 1972. OK-TEA is shown here making one of its rare appearances at London-Heathrow in June 1969.

Right:
According to CSA, the airline sold their two Tu-124s to Iraq in 1974, thus OK-TEA and OK-UEC became YI-AEL and YI-AEY. Sightings of these two aircraft have been few and far between and they seem to have disappeared after 1980. YI-AEY is seen on a visit to Warsaw in September 1978, possibly in connection with the purchase of the Mi-2 helicopters.

The Chinese Air Force operated three Tu-124s as VIP transports. These rare aircraft were never seen outside China during their twenty-one years of service from 1965 to 1986. Around 1980 the three Tu-124s were relegated to normal passenger work for military personnel owing to their replacement by three Tridents. 50257 had only just been withdrawn from use in 1987 at Nanyuan where it is seen parked on the grass. This aircraft over the next few years was moved around Nanyuan's large wooded aerodrome several times before it was finally despatched to Datang Shan Museum, Changping in 1993.

Above:

The basic short fuselage Tu-134s of which seventy-eight were built all fall into the catagory of vintage airliners as none of this type remain in service in the 1990s. The early Tu-134s, easily identifiable by their short tail bullets and glazed noses, first flew in 1963, entered Aeroflot service in 1967 and by 1990 were museum exhibits or dumped in a far corner of an airfield to rot away. Aeroflot operated forty-four examples, most of which found their way into the airports of western Europe during the late 1960s and early 1970s wearing their original Aeroflot colours. CCCP-65612 stands proud on the ramp at London-Heathrow Airport on a beautiful sunny Friday in May 1969. This aircraft was substituting for a Tu-104 on the once-weekly Leningrad-London route. This actual aircraft was operated throughout its life by Aeroflot's Leningrad Directorate, who were also responsible for the aircraft being broken up for scrap at Leningrad (now St Petersburg) in 1991.

Interflug were a big user of the Tu-134 range and initially flew eight of the short versions to neighbouring eastern bloc countries. By 1986 all eight aircraft had been despatched to museums and scrapyards with the exception of DM-SCA and DM-SCD which were early casualities in accidents at Dresden in 1972 and Leipzig in 1975 respectively. DM-SCD in its original form awaits its next flight at Berlin-Schönefeld Airport in August 1972. Three years later, this actual aircraft crashed short of the runway at Leipzig and was totally destroyed, killing all onboard.

Opposite Below:
During the 1970s, the operators of the Tu-134s modified the tail bullets to a long pointed fairing like the Tu-134As and by 1975 most aircraft had been sighted with this modification including the Aeroflot aircraft. Somehow, CCCP-65611 escaped the modification and is seen at Leningrad-Pulkovo Airport as late as August 1978 in its original form and the new Aeroflot colour scheme adopted in 1975, making this picture quite unique. CCCP-65611 has not been reported for many years and one can assume that it was broken up for scrap during the 1980s or suffered a crash.

Above:
Malév of Hungary operated seven Tu-134s of the short variety all of which were used on short-haul routes within east and west Europe between 1968 and 1988. Three examples, HA-LBA, HA-LBC and HA-LBD all crashed early in their lives and were replaced with the stretched and modified Tu-134As. HA-LBA is pictured here at London-Heathrow Airport in May 1969 with the regular Friday afternoon Aeroflot Tu-104 standing behind. In November 1969 HA-LBA overran the runway on landing at Istanbul in heavy rain and was subsequently destroyed.

Above:
Balkan flew seven early model Tu-134s throughout Europe. The first two examples, LZ-TUA and LZ-TUB, were delivered during September 1968 in the blue TABSO colours and by the end of 1969 were incorporated into the Balkan fleet of red-coloured Tu-134s. One month after delivery, LZ-TUB is parked at London-Heathrow Airport during its two-hour turn-around awaiting its return flight to Sofia.

LZ-TUB in its early Balkan red colours
approaches Berlin-Schönefeld Airport in
August 1972. Six years later in March
1978, LZ-TUB stalled at 10,000 feet after
take-off from Sofia. All seventy-three
onboard perished.

Above:
Five short Tu-134s were purchased by LOT for their European routes. They were first delivered in 1968. SP-LGB was the only casualty of the five basic Tu-134s when in January 1980 it overshot the runway at Warsaw-Okecie Airport, slammed into a dyke, caught fire and burnt out. The aircraft is seen in better days at Copenhagen-Kastrup waiting for take-off in June 1971

Above:
The Yugoslav tour operator Aviogenex operated three basic Tu-134s and nine Tu-134As. The three early versions, YU-AHH, YU-AHI and YU-AHS, were short-lived with Aviogenex. They were delivered in 1969 and returned to the Soviet Union in 1971 in exchange for the stretched Tu-134As. On a cold and wet September day in 1969, YU-AHH waits on the rain-soaked Manchester apron for its sixty-four passengers eager to climb onboard for a holiday in the Adriatic sun.

No other aircraft in the world creates such interest as a supersonic airliner of which only two types exist: Concorde and the Tu-144. Both types fall into two distinct catagories, Concorde is a highly successful airliner now enjoying over twenty years of commercial service and still going strong; the Tu-144 on the other hand can only be described as the world's biggest high tech political supersonic disaster.

The Russians were prompted to get involved in a supersonic commercial airliner as soon as they knew Great Britain and France had signed an agreement to share the massive development costs and produce such an airliner. The seed was sown on a Crimean beach near the home of Nikita Khrushchev at a secret meeting between Khrushchev, Andrei Tupolev, his son Alexei and a few other senior aviation and Government officials. According to the archives now available, Khrushchev demanded that the Soviet design must be better than Concorde and furthermore, the Tu-144 had to fly before Concorde. The KGB aviation department were told of their task and almost immediately the spies got to work on infiltrating the Anglo-French system to gather information. After the KGB had gathered all the basic information from the West, the 'need-to-know people' were informed. For the next seven years the Russians worked tirelessly to obtain information. During this period many Russian 'diplomats' fell foul of the western system and were subsequently expelled from either Great Britain or France on the grounds of industrial espionage.

The biggest problem for the Russian engineers was the engines; however, by some means a prototype was built. The year before the prototype flew, Khrushchev was deposed as party leader in 1967 and Leonid Brezhnev took over the top job in the Kremlin. Brezhnev increased research and development into the Tu-144 and on the last day of 1968 the Tu-144 took to the air, thus beating Concorde by three months.

The prototype, CCCP-68001, went into hiding for thirty months before it appeared at the 1971 Paris Air Show. Engineers from Great Britain and France took a close look at the Tu-144 and declared it to be an engineering nightmare that needed extensive modifications before it was capable of carrying passengers. CCCP-68001 appeared again in the West at the 1972 Hannover Air Show extensively modified, but still looking like a well-used 'second-hand' airliner. After this show in 1972, CCCP-68001 was never seen or heard of again.

Reports were drifting out of the Soviet Union that the new Tu-144 was ready to appear at the 1973 Paris Air Show and sure enough a pre-production version arrived from Moscow in the form of CCCP-77102. On taking one quick look at the aircraft and its two cannards (retractable wings) behind the cockpit windows, you do not need to be an aviation designer to realise that this machine has got problems with stability at low speed. The Paris Air Show of 1973 was to be the worst one in aviation history for the Russians. They suffered a major setback whilst the eyes of the world's best-known shop window witnessed the crash of CCCP-77102 whilst performing a tight turn. The crash killed all onboard, killed Aeroflot's enthusiasm for the project and destroyed Soviet pride.

From 1973 to 1977, extensive testing took place both experimentally and on passenger routes carrying cargo. CCCP-77109 eventually flew the first passenger service from Moscow to Alma Ata in November 1977. Six months later in May 1978, CCCP-77111 was operating a commercial passenger flight between Moscow and Khabarovsk when it had to make an emergency landing, reportedly caused by a fire onboard which has never been confirmed. The aircraft was so badly damaged that it could not be repaired. Even Aeroflot complained of the dangers and refused to have anything to do with this supersonic disaster. Early in June 1978, the Tu-144 was officially withdrawn from use and the project scrapped after 102 commercial passenger flights. So ends the Soviet Union's love affair with supersonic passenger flying.

CCCP-68001 the original prototype stands proud at Paris-Le Bourget in June 1971. From this view of the aircraft it is interesting to see how far back under the fuselage the nosewheel leg is situated, giving the appearance of being tail heavy.

CCCP-77102 passes the camera for the last time. After it banked over the air show grounds it flew into cloud and banked to the left . . . and that was the end . . .